A Day in the Life: Polar Animals

Arctic Fox

Katie Marsico

www.raintreepublishers.co.uk
Visit our website to find out more information about Raintree books.

To order:
☎ Phone 0845 6044371
🖷 Fax +44 (0) 1865 312263
🖳 Email myorders@raintreepublishers.co.uk

Customers from outside the UK please telephone +44 1865 312262

Raintree is an imprint of Capstone Global Library Limited, a company incorporated in England and Wales having its registered office at 7 Pilgrim Street, London, EC4V 6LB – Registered company number: 6695582

Edited by Daniel Nunn, Rebecca Rissman, and Sian Smith
Designed by Joanna Hinton-Malivoire
Picture research by Hannah Taylor
Original illustrations © Capstone Global Library
Production by Victoria Fitzgerald
Originated by Capstone Global Library Ltd
Printed and bound in China by South China Printing Company Ltd

ISBN 978 1 406 22882 3 (hardback)
15 14 13 12 11
10 9 8 7 6 5 4 3 2 1

British Library Cataloguing in Publication Data

Marsico, Katie, 1980-
  Arctic fox. -- (A day in the life. Polar animals)
  1. Arctic fox--Juvenile literature.
  I. Title II. Series
  599.7'764-dc22

Acknowledgements

We would like to thank the following for permission to reproduce photographs: Alamy Images pp. 8, 23b (© Arcticphoto), 10, 23a (© Dmitry Deshevykh), 11, 23g (© Dmitry Deshevykh), 15, 23c (© All Canda Photos), 18 (© Terry Whittaker); Corbis pp. 4, 23f (Science Faction/ Steven Kazlowski), 14 (Radius Images), 16 (Joe McDonald). 22 (Science Faction/Steven Kazlowski); FLPA p. 5 (Minden Pictures / Michio Hoshino); istockphoto p. 23e (© Tobias Johansson); naturepl.com p. 21 (Wild Wonders of Europe/de la Lez); Photolibrary pp. 6 (age fotostock/ Morales Morales), 12 (Superstock/Tom Brakefield), 17 (OSF/Richard Kemp), 19 (Tips Italia/ Bildagentur RM); Shutterstock pp. 7 (© Witold Kaszkin), 9 (© Witold Kaszkin), 13 (© Thomas Barrat), 20, 23d (© ecoventurestravel).

Cover photograph of an Arctic fox (Alopex lagopus) with its white winter coat reproduced with permission of Alamy (© WILDLIFE GmbH). Back cover photographs reproduced with permission of Shutterstock: hole (© Thomas Barrat), den (© ecoventurestravel).

The publisher would like to thank Michael Bright for his assistance in the preparation of this book.

Every effort has been made to contact copyright holders of material reproduced in this book. Any omissions will be rectified in subsequent printings if notice is given to the publisher.

Disclaimer

Contents

Some words are shown in bold, **like this**.
You can find them in the glossary on page 23.

What is an Arctic fox?

An Arctic fox is a **mammal** that lives in snowy areas.

All mammals have some hair on their bodies and feed their babies milk.

Arctic foxes are about the size of small dogs.

The colour of their fur helps them to **blend in** and hide.

What do Arctic foxes look like?

In the autumn and winter, Arctic foxes have thick, white fur.

Their fur matches the colour of the snow and keeps them warm.

In the spring and summer, Arctic foxes have grey or brown fur.

Arctic foxes also have a bushy tail and furry feet.

Where do Arctic foxes live?

Arctic

Arctic foxes live in a part of the world called the **Arctic**.

In the Arctic it is light all day and all night for part of the summer.

In the Arctic it is dark all day and all night for part of the winter.

The Arctic is one of the coldest and windiest places on Earth!

What do Arctic foxes do at night?

Arctic foxes are **nocturnal**.

This means they are usually more **active** at night.

Arctic foxes often spend part of the night hunting for food.

They have an excellent sense of smell that helps them to hunt in the dark.

What do Arctic foxes eat?

hare

Arctic foxes mainly eat **lemmings**.

They also hunt voles, hares, and nesting birds.

Arctic foxes sometimes look for scraps left over by larger animals, such as polar bears.

Many dig holes in the ground where they bury food to eat later.

What hunts Arctic foxes?

wolf

Polar bears and wolves hunt Arctic foxes.

Other types of foxes also attack and kill them.

People hunt Arctic foxes for their thick fur.

Arctic foxes sometimes escape their enemies by **blending in** with their surroundings.

Do Arctic foxes live in groups?

Arctic foxes live alone from late autumn to early spring.

They spend time in family groups for the rest of the year.

A group of Arctic foxes is called a skulk or a leash.

These groups are usually made up of 2 or 3 adults, and 3 to 12 babies.

What do Arctic foxes do in the day?

Arctic foxes are usually less **active** during the day.

They might spend some of this time resting.

Arctic foxes go hunting when the animals they want to eat are awake.

If those animals are awake in the day, then Arctic foxes sometimes hunt during the day.

What are baby Arctic foxes like?

den

Baby Arctic foxes are called kits or pups and they are born inside **dens**.

Baby foxes look like small versions of their parents.

Kits start hunting when they are about 14 weeks old.

They soon learn how to survive outside the den in the frosty **Arctic**!

Arctic fox body map

fur

tail

foot

mouth

Glossary

active busy doing lots of things

Arctic area surrounding the North Pole. It is very cold in the Arctic.

blend in to match the colours of the surroundings and be hard to spot

den hole in the ground where Arctic foxes sleep and give birth to their babies

lemming small, mouse-like animal with a short tail

mammal animal that feeds its babies milk. All mammals have some hair or fur on their bodies.

nocturnal awake and active at night

Find out more

Books
Arctic and Antarctic (Eye Wonder), Lorie Mack (DK Publishing, 2006)
Arctic Foxes, Maeve Sisk (Gareth Stevens Publishing, 2010)

Websites
www.defenders.org/wildlife_and_habitat/wildlife/arctic_fox.php
Find out about the Arctic fox on the Defenders of Wildlife website.

animals.nationalgeographic.com/animals/mammals/arctic-fox/
Learn more about the Arctic fox with National Geographic.

Index